GOD TO GOD

PATRICIA A. DAVID

Copyright © 2020 by Patricia A. David

All rights reserved. This book or any portion thereof may not be reproduced or transmitted in any form or manner, electronic or mechanical, including photocopying, recording, or by any information storage or retrieval system, without the express written permission of the copyright owner except for the use of brief quotations in a book review or other noncommercial uses permitted by copyright law.

Printed in the United States of America

Library of Congress Control Number:		2020915341
ISBN:	Softcover	978-1-64908-252-7
	Hardback	978-1-64908-253-4
	eBook	978-1-64908-251-0

Republished by: PageTurner Press and Media LLC
Publication Date: 08/26/2020

To order copies of this book, contact:

PageTurner Press and Media
Phone: 1-888-447-9651
order@pageturner.us
www.pageturner.us

God to God

And when he had sent the multitude away, he went up into a mountain privately to pray, and when the evening was come, he was there alone.

Matt 17 : 23

And it came to pass in those days, that he went out into a mountain to pray, and continued all night in prayer to God.

Luke 6 : 12

I have glorified thee on the earth; I have finished the work which thou gavest me to do.

John 17 : 4

Introduction

The intent of this book and the others I have written is to spread the joy of the Lord to know Him. To rejoice in peace, grace, love, rest and knowledge of what God has done for us. And to reach those who do not know Him by writing these poems for them to read and receive the gift of His love. I have been writing poems for many years with the encouragement of my mother. Some poems have scriptures with them please read the scriptures and find Him.

Time with God

I do not wish the day be through
      but that I speak you.
For day and night come from Thee,
      and all the beauty that I see.
Comfort comes from Your loving hands,
      all within Your Loving plan.
Salvation within your death for me,
      across the world so vast and free
Let mankind be drawn to your Loving care,
      and we shall meet You in the air.
Come up heather will be Your cry,
      when we will asend up in the sky.
Prepare our hearts for when You come again,
      and loose these bodies from our sin,
And Heaven's Gates to enter in,
      Praise the Father and praise His Son.
      for Jesus makes the whole world One.

Apr. 2020

God's Last Call

Hasten, oh hasten to the Master's call,
    for it may be the last one we can hear at all.
Other voices all around us that would draw our souls away,
    so come to Jesus come to Jesus while you may.
We can't boast about tomorrow for tomorrow may never come,
    If God is pulling your heart strings, don't turn away like some.
Today is the day of salvation for ours soul,
    Jesus can cleanse you and make you whole.

                        Oct. 2, 2016

Love and Peace

What God is allows to come into our lives is for our training and growth.
That we would learn to draw on Him and His strength not relying on our own.
It's to prepare us to be ready for our eternal home.
Inside Heaven's door, we will want no more to roam

Apr. 2020

Check Your Heart

Secrets, secrets, and secrets, we might tell them every day,
    sometimes we don't tell anyone, we just hide them away.
Some live within a pretend world where its beautiful and bright,
    but when they search their heart, they know things are not right.
For days and weeks and sometimes years, they live in their despair,
    being as one that beateth the air.
Not knowing which way to go to get them through,
    trust Jesus Christ for He is true,
So then we run the race to win,
    but only can we do it because of Him.

Oct. 2, 2016

God holds our Tomorrow

Laugh out loud, to feel free within,
    to know that you are free from sin.
Let your heart leap for joy,
    no longer Satan's toy.
Catch a glimpse of heaven's view,
    made for me and made for you.
Be comforted in your soul,
    for God has made you whole.
So laugh out loud once again,
    turn to Satan with a grim.
For God holds your destiny,
    for all eternity.

Feb. 27, 2013

Rapture Day

Beyond tomorrow or perhaps today,
    Jesus is coming to take His love ones away.
Then in His presents we will always stay,
    no more sin to burden each day.
Then God will watch His children play,
    no restrictions to bar their way.
In God's presents we will rejoice,
    listen to God's dear sweet voice.
Not afraid of man or beast,
    for now to dwell in perfect peace.

June 8, 2020

Not Adrift

Sun over the ocean, moon over the sea,
    before I knew I was drifting, the Savior was watching me.
Gently He turned my life around and guided me across the wide expanse,
    into the narrow harbor without a backward glance.
I feel His presents daily wherever I should roam,
    but I know that I'll not be truly happy until I arrive at home.

Sept. 29, 2013

Dwelling Place

God gave the sun to light our way,
    as we go about from day to day.
God gave His Son to pay for our sins,
    there was no other way to bring peace within.
For if our souls in Jesus Christ abides,
    we are truly made alive.
Times on earth are changing fast,
    soon we shall dwell with Christ at last.

Sept. 29, 2013

Earthly Pleasures

Earth may have it's pleasures and joys as down here we do travel,
    but without the Lord our lives would quickly unravel.
So set your sights on Christ today,
    and in His Word He'll lead the way.
And whether waves or currents tall,
    learn that Christ is your all and all.

Sept. 27, 2013

Millions

If I had a million life times and could spread cheer to every face,
    it would be for nothing without God's amazing grace.
To make your heart pure,
    come and trust in Jesus and your soul will be made sure.
Eternal life in Christ is endless joy forever more,
    we're waiting now for our Lord God to open heaven's door.
Don't argue with the Holy Spirit who wants to save your soul,
    let Him come into your life and make you fully whole.
Then join with me to ring out an eternal cry,
    look to God in heaven before life ends and you die.

                                                  Nov, 13, 2014

Desert

As we walk across the desert sands, seeking for a far off land.
Parched our eyes and throats are dry, within our spirit we let out a cry.
    Where oh, where is the water supply?
Then from that still small voice within, drink from my well and never thirst again.
I dipped into the clear cool waters of God's love,
    that made me ready for Heaven above.
Don't just stand there lost in sin, search the scriptures, jump in.

Sept. 29, 2013

Perfect Peace

Did you ever think that the day would,
      come when peace would fill the world.
Gone away are hate and sin no longer to dwell within,
      all our nights will be turned to day,
As in God's presents there to stay,
      celestial homes fill the way.
Then all will be perfectly well,
      for with God we will eternally dwell.

Lord of Lords

Listening for the call of God in your life,
    learning to wait on Christ's Word to take away strife.
Loving to fellowship with God and of like faith,
    leaning on Jesus and sharing His perfect grace.
Leading others to spread the Word,
    laughing with those who trusted God, when they heard.
Longing for Heaven and those gone before,
    looking for signs that Christ is at the door.
Listening for the trumpet to announce the Wedding Day,
    leaving for heaven with God to stay.

Mar. 25, 2014

While He is Close

Have you ever had the thought that life is not right,
    and for you the future is not bright?
The Holy Spirit deals with us to draw us to the Lord's new life,
    Turn your heart to God today and draw near to His call.
repent your sins and ask Him to dwell once and for all,
    Christ died to save both big and small.
no matter your background His call goes to all.

" Seek ye the Lord while He may be found, call ye upon Him while He is near."
Isaiah 55:6

Aug. 26, 2014

For Who?

As I stand beneath Your Cross and think of what you have done,
    God's only begotten Son.
Jesus, You took my place,
    and not mine only but for the whole human race.

June 1, 2020

Say What?

When times at time are weary and long may seem the day,
    look around you and take notice that people go the same way.
When you get to the age to take care of yourself, we have no one else to blame,
    for lives that are different are still the same.

June 1, 2020

Patience

Patience is not easy in times of testing in our life,
      for if we pray for patience, then God sometimes allows more strife.
      you only learn through falling, how to walk in this life,
So pray for God's Grace to keep you true,
      to keep you through each hurtle, He brings you thru,
As we look back on our journey both the good times and the bad,
      knowing that God is always beside us, makes us, oh so glad.

                                                  Apr. 26, 2014

Day by Day

Tenderly He welcomes me each time I call His name,
He's always there to share my cares to comfort not to blame
. He knows each thought I think, each word I'm about to say,
But by my side God still abides, and loves me day by day,
My life is anchored in His Word My feet planted on the Rock of Ages.
Faithful and true His Words to the sages.

Apr.11, 2013

What We Owe God

We walk in God's encouragement as we travel here below,
    read His Word and know Him and how He loves so.
That the more we draw close to Him and watch His helping hand,
    that what He does and what He said are part of His plan.
For as we travel through His Word and dwell within His care,
    we start to realize all was written for us to share.
To learn to know the mind of Christ, it becomes our very life,
    it stirs our soul to realize only He take away our strife.
Don't borrow cares from tomorrow, let tomorrow be a surprise,
    Give our days unto the Lamb to whom we owe our lives.

Mar. 2, 2014

Beautiful Savior Jesus

Christ's name is Beautiful, Beautiful, say it again and again
Christ's love us so yes loves so, that to the old rugged cross He would go.
Now in the end of time it will be sublime for with Him we will know.
How we can love Him more than we did before, and see Him face to face.
He's the one who died for us to set our spirit free for all Eternity.

May 1, 2020

Can't Be Too Soon

Holy, Holy, are You Lord God Almighty
      I will sing forth Your praises thru all eternity
As I seek Your face each morning I will feed upon Your Word.
      Lead me to Your Sanctuary as I come to worship You.
I find strength within Your Wondrous Love and Care.
Give me grace to share Your gift of salvation to those I come in contact with,
There are so many needy who need a touch from You.
Open wide my eyes that I may see them and encourage them to invite
You in to abide. Like a light from a lighthouse may Your Word ever shine.
Thank you Lord for Your loving kindness to me you have bestowed,
And someday soon, I will be there to worship You upon Your throne.

                                                   Nov. 9, 2013

Wedding Day

Look up, look up, to the sky and pray, even so come quickly Lord Jesus may it be today.

Closer still closer the time is drawing near, when our precious Savior shall appear.

We'll hear the trumpet sound, and we will leave the ground.

Upward we will fly to meet our bridegroom in the sky.

What rejoicing there will be, when our Savior we will see.

Oct. 26, 2013

Redeemer

Jesus I thank you for dying for me,
    and with your Precious Blood you set me free.
For everlasting and eternally you will ever be,
    the One who brought me from darkness so I could see.
Caused me to walk on solid ground for eternity,
    keep me in your Word each day so I truly will be.
And hold me close to Thee for all eternity.

" Let the Words of my mouth and the meditation of my heart, be acceptable in Thy sight, O Lord my Strength, and my Redeemer "
Palms 19: 14

Grow Up

Jesus is knocking at your heart's door, oh won't you let Him come in ?
Remember that Jesus died for you, so a new life you can begin.
Not by works that we have done to try to get to Glory,
      but by the blood that Jesus shed for you, that's the end of God's story.
Our happiness is in the Lord and by His Words we grow,
      some grow fast, some grow slow but all that really matters is to grow.

                                            Feb. 15, 2020

Rest in God

Rest will come in the morning when I see your Blessed Face.
    then I will truly know your amazing grace.
All the earth will shout with joy, more than when the earth began.
For we will be blessed always by Your Mighty Hand,
    bless you Heavenly Father and Your Holy Son.
    bless your Holy Spirit, the Great three in one.
Let us not grow weary as we wait for that glad day.
    let us remember God is only a prayer away.

Feb. 15, 2020

Praise to You

Father, I praise you for who you are, your wisdom is too much for me.
Your love is beyond our understanding, your presents I know is with me.
You who created the universe, you put all things in motion.
I love you not like I should, please forgive me, Lord, for all the times I let you down.
Open my eyes to those with special needs,
Open my mouth and give me your words of wisdom.
Let me not draw upon my own strength, but constantly rely on Yours.
For in my strength I will but fail. My victory is in You, my Lord and Savior

Feb. 15, 2020

Higher and Higher

We know that trials will come along each day,
    so draw close to God and read His Word, and come what may.
Satan loves to tease us to stray. Call out to Jesus,
    claim His blood and Satan will crawl away.
Christ's blood is the strongest thing we have against each foe.
    and the devil is defeated and will have to go.
Don't let him have the victory that Jesus promised you.
    rest in God's Word and be lifted to heights anew.

Feb. 14, 2020

Life's Tapestry

Life is like a tapestry, we only from one side do view,
      with reveling yarn and cut ragged ends, nothing looks brand new.
We are a work in progress from beginning to end
      we only see the backside, for we are the blend.
For life is sometimes messy and sometimes very sad,
      but if we trust God the Father, the life rug will make us glad.
Jesus sees the front side with its beauty and its light,
      He will show us the beauty that comes out of our night.
To see our lives thus fashioned by the Master's patient hands,
      to know that from the beginning, we were in His plans.

" For now we see in a mirror darkly; but then, face to face; now I know in part, But then shall I know even as also I am known."
1 Con. 13:12

                                                            Feb. 19, 2020

Whisper A Prayer

Whisper a prayer in the morning to begin the day off right.
Whisper a prayer before you read God's Word, to make His Word your light.
Whisper a prayer before you share God's word,
    that the Holy Spirit would touch their heart and life.
Whisper a prayer, as you prepare for whatever task you have to do.
Whisper a prayer for things He provides - friends, family, work and home too.
Beauty of the earth, and sunsets when each day is done.
But most of all, give thanks to God for giving us His Son .
And with each prayer, we know He's there all along the way.
In the morning and at the close of every day.

                                                  Sept. 24, 2010

Jesus the Reason

Whisper a prayer to begin the day.
    Read God's Word and don't forget to pray.
        Ask Him to guide you and lead you along.
            Praise Him as He gives you a song
God gave His Son, Jesus, to die in our place.
    That's where we see God's amazing grace.
        Jesus is the reason we celebrate each day.
            To know He leads along the narrow way.

                        Feb. 14, 2020

Protective

The Lord is my protector, I walk along His side.
    and thru the years, I 've learned to hear and abide.
He's loving and gracious and always kind,
    and if I couldn't see it I would be blind. He is One of a kind.

                                                          Feb. 14, 2020

Listen for the Call

He is coming to catch us away
    Oh praise God for that blesses day
The trumpet shall be sounded
    And upward we are bounded.
Our sins completely wiped away,
    As with Christ Jesus we will stand
Play trumpet for the Bridegroom cometh and nothing shall delay,
    And who knows it could be today

Oct. 16, 2016

Inspired

Within the mind of mortal man, leaves little to be inspired.
> for mankind's thoughts are prone to wander and much to be desired.

If mankind's thoughts would dwell on God, they would be uplifted.
> but instead, alas, they are controlled by Satan and by his thoughts are sifted.

For in this flesh, we run here and there in sin, and turn around,
> run the same way again.

Let's look to God for clarity within our lives to live and pray to God,
> for wisdom which He will surely give.

No vast realm of knowledge could we dwell upon each day,
> then what our Heavenly Father has prepared for us to learn along the way.

Be prepared to meet life's test each day,
> when things get tough, go to our God and pray.

For Jesus paid for our sacrifice in His body alone,
> so that you and I can worship our Lord seated on His throne.

May 8, 2014

God's Dear Child

God gave His beloved Son to die,
    to take the Sins of you and I.
God could not look on Christ that final hour,
    because He had our sins placed on Him to give us power.
Power to be forgiven for our sins,
    the only way that all people would win.
Christ's blood covers us and can keep us from Satan's wiles,
    that's because when we commit to Jesus we are then God's child.

                        Jan. 13, 2013

Ten Little Words

When we try to get through this life on our own,
    we forget God sees us from His Heavenly Throne.
Satan binds our hearts and minds to do his will,
    to get us deeper in sin, gives him a real thrill.
Ten little words can upset him and ruin his day,
    <u>Lord forgive me and make me Your Own to stay.</u>

Jan. 13, 2017

Home at Last

When on this earth my footsteps last stand,
    my feet will be walking in Heaven's land.
Where with those who have trusted in the Lord Jesus Christ will be,
    At last and always for eternity.
That precious day can't be too soon for me,
    to see my Lord who died to set me free .
Blessed hope is free to all those who trust in Jesus,
    the Only One who died to free us.
Now that I stand and wait my turn,
    I yearn to sit at Jesus' feet and learn.
Loved ones who have gone on before,
    will welcome me beyond Heaven's door,
No tears up there to blind my way,
    for with Christ Jesus I will be home to stay.

Nov. 26, 2016

LIFE

Life is like a water fall,
      giving drink to one and all.
Rushed may be the path we trod,
      hope that stirs our hearts to God.
Long may seems each day ahead,
      hold onto God's hand and pray instead.

But whosoever drinketh of the water that I shall give him shall never thirst; But the water that I shall give him shall be in him a well of water springing up Into everlasting life.
John 4:1

Jesus Walks With Me

Truthful, truthful, rest beneath your wings,
        and while I lay upon your Holy Breast I lift my voice and sing.
Melody, sweet melody throughout my night are filled and with each breath,
        my longing heart reaches for eternal rest.
For Jesus ' blood paid for my sin and in my life I know,
        His promises are as true today as they were so long ago.
In life or death, He holds my hand and leads me along life's way,
        and very soon His face I'll see to wipe all tears away.
        Help me walk beside you,
Lead me with your precious Word every day, every day
        And help me humbly pray.
When at the close of this life,
        take me home, where there is no more strife.

" I will never leave thee, nor forsake thee."
Heb. 13:5b

        Oct. 30, 2016

Feeling His Presents

Father, I love You, You are so good and **kind,**
 And I know that You are truly **mine.**
As You shower me,, with blessing from **above,**
 I want to be lost, in the wonder of Your **love.**
Each new blessing from You I hold so **dear,**
 And I feel Your presents is so near to comfort and **cheer.**

Apr. 30, 2013

How not to start the Day

I jumped out of bed one day,
    and said to myself it's a brand new day.
To get things done and then to play, but right away things went so wrong,
    and the day would drag on oh, so long.
Then I stopped and sat awhile
    and to my face there came a smile,
Then the Spirit spoke to me, that the best way to start the day
    is with the Lord and a time to pray.
Remember, yes remember do,
    and know that God's word is true.

Nov. 21, 2012

In Praise

Sitting together before God's Throne,
> this is the day that we are looking forward to and shall be known.

God's Word has told us and told again the things in His Word that were made clear,
> oh, that I wish that all would really hear.

The day of wrath is at the door,
> trust in Christ, let your life truly Him adore.

May God's Word be the end of sin's reign,
> let your heart be covered with Christ's blood stain

Spread His Word let it be shared,
> don't just sit there but let God's Word be given forth in prayer

His Name

Come and see,
        the one who died for me.
After He had been placed in the grave,
        He came back to life, and new life He gave.
You've heard His Words and know His name,
        Jesus Christ our Lord took all our blame.
Reach out to Him and ask Him in to take your sins away,
        Don't wait another day.

" behold, now is the day of salvation."
2 Cor. 6:2b

Oct. 15, 2016

Open Your Ears

You have heard God's Words, will you ever draw near?
He knocks at your heart's door when will you hear?
You know something is missing in your life,
Each day is filled with sorrow and strife.
Open your heart to Christ today.
Make Him part of your life while you may.

Oct. 15, 2016

Ordinary People

Ordinary people can have their dreams come true,
    If they put their trust in Christ for their whole life through.
They can travel through this life,
    Free from guilt and strife.
Waiting for their Heavenly home,
    No more to have to roam.

Oct. 15, 2016

Christ Alone

Repent, Repent the cry goes out today,
      soon the Lord will come to take His bride away.
Hope to all,
      remember how Satan had bound you, and you listened to Christ's call.
Put away earthly things that last for a short while,
      rest in Christ alone and His peace will make you smile,
Be cleanse from inside out by the blood of Christ alone,
      and know that someday very soon we'll see Him seated on His throne.

July 4, 2014

Sealed by God

God made the ocean, God made the sea, God made the universe and God made me.

God made each baby with a sweet little nose, ten little fingers and ten little toes.

Remember all this is God's plan, a way to replenish man.

Let's not turn our backs on God, as only men can.

Satan clouds our minds, and wants us to find, a replacement for God.

To fill our days, with this world's maze to center on ourselves.

But no matter with what we fill our lives, and answer we are still, hell-bent.

July 21, 2013

Trust In God

Jesus is the answer to the world today.
    but the world is busy moving the other way.
Sins are outwardly encouraged to be done,
    fully disrespecting the gift of God's Son.
How it must sadden the Holy God above,
    that the world reject the gift of God's love.
Not thinking about tomorrow just living for today,
    they do not realize or care that for their sin they'll pay.
Be faithful you know the Lord,
    share with those who need to hear of God's love in one accord.
That they not follow Satan on the downward path,
    but receive God's Word and put their trust in Him at last.

Dec. 22, 2012

His Sheep Am I

In God's green pastured feeding, by His cool waters lye,
    soft in the evening walk my Lord and I.
All the sheep of His pasture fair so wondrously find, His sheep am I
        Waters cool, pasture green, in the evening walk my Lord and I
            Dark the night, rough the way, steps my Lord and I.

Listening for God's Call

The grandeur of the earth below and stars scattered across the sky,
> can not compare to our home that God's preparing up on high.

The darkness of this sin cursed earth and all that hold it dear,
> will be swept away in God's own time, which could be very near.

For those who trust God loving gift, Christ Jesus is His name,
> we will be with God His Righteousness to claim.

There will be no memory of the sin that once was so terrible,
> but we will be dwelling in that great land, that not anywhere is comparable.

Each Step

Quite my spirit Lord as I start a brand new <u>day,</u>
    let it be filled with joy as I pass along this <u>way.</u>
May my life touch others with Your life <u>anew,</u>
    cause their hearts be turned to Jesus so they can trust You <u>too.</u>
Let the breath that You have given me be not wasted on <u>regrets,</u>
    may I dwell instead in Your great Gift and in Your present <u>sit.</u>
Let me feel Your strong arm lift me, as I travel the hard <u>ways,</u>
    help me look to you Dear Lord, each step of <u>everyday.</u>

                                                          July 8, 2013

Heavy Laden

When darkness crowds around you and fear is everywhere,
    and life is full of endless care.
When each step you take is heavy, an each breath is labored too.
    when your life has become sorrowful, let me share what to do.
Call on Jesus to release you from the load of sin you bear,
    call on Jesus to take away each and every care.
Now pray and thank Jesus for He has set you free,
    then tell others of a glorious eternity.
The Blood shall set you free,
    then share how Christ has saved you and set you free.

Oct. 26, 2016

Coming Soon

There is coming a day, when all pain will pass away.
Sin will draw it's final breath at last, trouble and trial will all be past.
Sing out my soul to the One who died for me, praise Lord Jesus who set me free.
Be ever mindful of the coming King, and of the justice He will bring.
Let your light so shine, the Lord God will be the sign.
That the night will be turned into day, and all death will be wiped away.

Be Prepared

Oh, God, I thank You for Your _Love_, that sent Your Son Jesus from _above_.
To wrap His arms around sinners like _I,_ to show us Your Love and then _die._
But He did not stay dead Oh No!, you _See,_ He rose from the grave for you and _me._
Because His love is strong and _pure._ It holds us in His Hand safe and _secure._
So till that day when God's trumpet _sounds,_ and our feet will leave the _ground._
Be faithful through the days be _long,_ but dwell on God, He will give you a _song._
Jesus by the Holy Spirit teach us to _pray,_
    and keep us watching for that blessed _Day._

" Even so Come Quickly Lord Jesus "
Rev. 22:20

June 22, 2015

Looking Upward

Lord, help me walk in Your Spirit of Love,
        fill me with Your wisdom from above.
Let me bask in wonders of Your Word,
        bring into my life those who haven't heard
May I share Your love with those along my way.
        open hearts to You , I fervently pray
Faithful You have always been,
        it's wonderful to know You are my friend.
Prepare me for the tests, that come my way
        let me come before Your present in prayer each day.
May I hold unto Your nail scared hand,
        and praise You for Your loving plan.
Then at the end of my journey here, I'll stand within the gates of the Promise Land.
        where peace will be, forever more on that perfect golden shore.

                                        Apr. 15, 2013

Gods Promises

God has not promised us an apple *a day*,
when we seek Him to provide our daily bread and *pray*.
When we pray to God, He already knows our *heart*,
And if we fully trust Him and had from the very *start.*
God has not promised to give us all that we *desire*,
Sometimes He chooses us to walk thru the *fire*
But when we trust Him fully each step of our *way*,
God is with us each and every *day*
Hear me now with both of your *ears*,
Let God's Word be your reaching through out all your *years.*

June 12, 2016

Only Believe

Why must our heart not believe, unless a miracle that we see.

For we know that Christ alone, is the only one who can lead us home.

For our real home is not on earth, but through Christ we have our second birth.

For do we only seek God in times of trail, when our hearts can not smile.

For when each step we take upon this earth, does not fill us with Heavenly mirth.

Check your heart just to see, if you've trusted Jesus is your plea.

Trust and obey for there's no other way, to be happy in Jesus than to trust and obey.

Forgive Me

Forgive me for the things I've said that made you want to cry
      forgive me for the things I've done for which you had to die.
I know that You forgive me when I called upon Your name,
      I know You came to die for me and take away my blame.
My sins were nailed to Your cross when You died in my place,
      not only my sins but for the whole human race.
So help us all remember Your tender love and care,
      that drove you to that rugged cross our sins to bare.

Dec. 6, 2015

Lead Me

Mighty are your arms oh Lord to hold me up each day.
You keep me safe within you love don't let me ever stray.
Prepare my heart for what's ahead, let me feel Your leading Lord
      and know that you have lead.

Lightning Source UK Ltd.
Milton Keynes UK
UKHW040928180920
370091UK00001BA/32